THE REBELLIOUS PLANET

Rev. Robert M. Blacmn
N.C.

A ZONDERVAN PAPERBACK

THE REBELLIOUS PLANET

by

LON WOODRUM

ZONDERVAN PUBLISHING HOUSE
GRAND RAPIDS, MICHIGAN

Appreciation is expressed to the Macmillan Co. for permission to quote from *The New Testament in Modern English* by J. B. Phillips, copyright 1958.

CONTENTS

THE REBELLIOUS PLANET

1. THE WAY THINGS ARE

"And that's the way things are — October, 1964," said a famous newscaster on television.

And things were not too good.

It was a troubled world. Revolutions and riots leaped up all over the earth. Crime was climbing at a frightening rate in the United States. Racial strife was boiling. The news was mostly bad.

Things weren't the way good folk wanted them to be. They weren't the way they should have been. But that's how they were.

The television newscast, of course, didn't cover the whole human story. Some good things were happening in the world also. Hungry kids were being fed. People were loving one another. Someone gave his life to help others. Men used their strength and intellects to discover a deterrent to human suffering.

Still, the bad news held the top place. Evil loomed large, if not terrifying, over the globe. Lawlessness was ascending. Hell seemed pushing for a real holiday.

It would be brash to say that there is more evil than good in the world. For we must never discount the power of good, since it is always positive, and evil is negative. Yet, let's face it: evil holds the spotlight, gets the headlines, sounds the loud trumpets.

Doubtless in a country such as the United States, only a minority of people believe in divorce, shrug off corruption in high places, or stand aloof from crime. Yet, at the rate we are traveling, it might not be too long until those who openly back evil and lawlessness may be in the majority! If this happens, heaven have mercy on our world!

We must confront the fact that there's a moving in the mulberry leaves toward the accommodation to wrong. More and more good people shy away from taking a stand against evil. We don't want to get "involved."

Of course, we give a "reason" for our withdrawal. Again and again we hear of people who rush in to help others and get hurt themselves. One man tried to help a woman whose husband was beating her without mercy, and after conking the husband, he wound up in jail. Some have tried to help injured persons, to be sued later for their pains. It's a crazy world.

Recently a drama on TV showed a man, who during an evening with his lady love in an illicit affair, witnessed a murder being committed. An innocent man was charged with the crime. Yet the protagonist knew that if he came forward and testified in behalf of the innocent man, he would jeopardize both his marriage and his job. The trial dragged on and the innocent man was convicted. Only then did the witness come forth and tell the truth. Everybody got excited over his "honesty," and they made him a big hero — for doing what any right-minded man should have done without taking a whole month to make up his mind about it! And, considering that the protagonist was engaged in an unsavory love affair, the theme of the drama seemed to be that the modern American has a tough time being decent about most anything!

Not long ago *Look* magazine ran an article with a black screaming caption: WHO CARES? The article repeated some of the now well-known cases of viciousness, such as the stabbing of Catherine Genovese while thirty-eight persons watched the grisly show without even calling the police. It retold the story of sixty persons watching a cop battle two murderous youths, crying for help, and getting none; of a New York crowd looking on while eight men stomped two others; of another crowd which refused to assist a girl being mistreated by a rapist.

We may get almost ill at hearing such stories over and over again — but that's the way things are!

Some writers refer to our metropolitan centers as "city jungles." Women, even men for that matter, may not be safe in our streets after dark, and in some streets not even in daylight. Riots and looting and burning increase.

Perhaps you have heard of the thirty-two couples in Sacramento, California, who were involved in a wife-swapping club. Some of them had to hire baby-sitters while they went about their swapping program! A detective discovered the setup, after being urged to the case by a newspaper woman; but all his labors were for nothing. The District Attorney's office shrugged the whole thing off, with, "A private exchange of spouses among consenting adults for temporary pleasure is not a crime. Wife swapping just doesn't violate any section of the penal code of California."

Then there was the case of many indictments of a grand jury against wives for part-time prostitution — who lived in split-level homes and whose husbands made good salaries. Husbands often baby-sat while their wives plied their trade! Thirty-nine persons in all were indicted. A policeman was involved, as were several "respectable" places of business.

According to *Newsweek* a blue-ribbon jury brought in 137 indictments, alleging 217 separate criminal actions, against some of the most powerful men in the state departments of eight states and Washington, D.C. Bribes, pay-off schemes, and other forms of skulduggery were named in the indictments.

That's how things are!

And how are things among the top echelons in our national capital — apart from the rumbling about the Bobby Baker case, that is? You have heard, we presume, of the scandal that was hushed up some time back — the one about what accommodations were made for Indonesia's President Sukarno during his visit to the United States. Seems a representative of the Indonesian embassy approached the State Department about securing women for Sukarno to keep him company in his travels about the land of the free and the home of the brave. He wanted several different types — evidently Mr. Sukarno is easily bored by any one type of woman! State Department officials, naturally, said they couldn't do anything — *officially*, that is! But a former FBI fellow was suggested, who was now a private eye. Mr. Private Eye agreed to get the girls for Mr. President, and did, according to the report. One wonders how many times the President of Indonesia broke the Mann Act while meandering about America with his temporary harem.

One wonders also how many other things are happening in Washington, and other places in this land, that have been hushed up even better than the Sukarno scandal.

And how are things going with the kids in the U.S.A.?

Not too well, we're afraid. Two hundred of them from Chicago's North Shore suburbs invaded a party in Winnetka and manhandled policemen who tried to drive them off. They pelted the cops with beer bottles and bricks. A newspaper editorial referred to these young folk as "a guerrilla army of punks." These kids were not from the slums. They came from expensive homes, and attended excellent schools. The woman whose party was invaded asked, "What are we going to do about these people?" The editor of a Chicago newspaper allowed he didn't know the answer to that, but that, before heaven, *something* should be done, before our country is wrecked!

Where the kids are from seems to make little difference — from well-to-do families and neighborhoods to those from ghettos, they're all ready for a nice destructive riot at the drop of a beer bottle! Geographically, it doesn't matter, either. Two gangs, numbering hundreds, ripped things apart generally in both New Hampshire and Oregon over a Labor Day weekend.

The kid's just aren't doing too well.

But that's the way things are.

Things aren't too nice in foreign countries, either. Over there the kids are acting up too. In England they have been on a real stomping spree. People get battered and kicked just for being handy when the kids feel like jumping up and down on somebody. The students riot in Japan, in Saigon, in Ankara, and all over. Rioting in the streets has become the pastime of youth in our generation.

Trouble in Cyprus, in South Viet Nam, in Indonesia, everywhere. Anything could happen in a world like ours — any time. The nuclear lid could blow off and leave our cities in poisonous dust. It's a dangerous world.

Bob Hope has referred to it as a "pressure-cooker

world." Billy Graham has said we are a planet in rebellion against God.

This doesn't sound too encouraging, I realize, and I brace myself for being dubbed as a topflight alarmist.

But that's the way things are!

So, how are things with the *Church?* This seems a fine time to set the Cross over against the boiling black clouds of trouble and evil. Time to make like those suffering, singing people in the journal of the primitive church, the Acts of the Apostles, and bring a flaming witness to a lost world. But what we are doing in many sections is losing members. And in 1962, the per capita giving of forty-one million church members for foreign missions was $2.16 for the year! Which means the average church member gave *four* cents a week for foreign missions! Which might also mean that if the average member was a cigarette smoker, at the same rate as his giving, he'd allow himself seven packs per annum; or if a beer-drinker, seven bottles!

This is disheartening news in the face of the commitment of communists to their unholy cause, we admit. We don't like to hear it any more than any one else. It leaves us sad, troubled, if not with somewhat of a defeatist attitude.

But that's the way things are!

2. THE EXPLOSIVE ERA

Ours is a time when vast revloutionary forces have been released across our planet, forces which it seems at times threaten to tear it part. New revolts keep breaking out over the world. And where there are no revolts there is uneasiness, unrest and symptoms of spiritual agony.

This has been called the age of technological revolution, and the age of the cybernetic revolution. It is an age when political and idealogical revolution and counter-revolution sweep about the globe.

There is revolution in society, education, culture and religion.

Max Lerner has even called ours *The Age of Overkill,* because of our frightening ability to deal enough death to more than destroy mankind!

This is the time of mighty *explosions.*

For one, there is the population explosion, which, according to some experts may well threaten the whole world — including the over-productive United States! — with dreadful famine. One economist has predicted that the U.S. may have many starving people by 1970!

We have an automation explosion. Machines leap into being, strange machines, even weird machines; machines that can speak and act and "think." And now we hear of machines that may reproduce themselves!

This giant thrust into automation results in another dark threat: that of unemployment for millions. A group of us clergymen were asked to meet with labor leaders in Akron, Ohio, to discuss this situation. We had many questions, but scarcely any answers at all. Automation still stared us in the face, offering problems we could not begin to solve.

Of all explosions in the troubled time none perhaps has made a mightier impact on us than that of the atom-explosion. Now the nations tremble lest the atom-storm blow and sweep away all our proud cities! An outstanding news magazine announced that the United States has enough nuclear power on hand to destroy both Russia and China in a matter of hours if she were disposed to use it.

Probably one of the biggest explosions is the way in which new nations have exploded into being.

When the old colonial powers began to crack up and break apart new countries were born. Many of these are yet locked in death struggles of civil war and revolt.

Recently the world watched how a new nation in Africa went wild and committed atrocities which left us shocked and afraid. And we have the feeling that the torturing and murdering of Christians in the Congo may well be but a prelude to a world persecution of God's people. Our mission fields have been closing for some time all about the earth. It may well be quite impossible for an American Christian missionary to go anywhere with the Gospel before long.

This is not, of course, to argue that the black savages

in the Congo are more, if as much, guilty as were the Nazis in their horrible mistreatment of the Jews a few years ago. We realize this when we recall how at Auschwitz, Germany, under Hitler's regime, the very earth was poisoned with the ashes of men, women and children who were destroyed by deadly gas.

We might well recall, too, the thirty years of terrorism of Stalin in Russia. Or we might think of the present beating and butchering of Negroes in certain parts of the United States!

But there are certain aspects of Africa which are too dark to be ignored. Once we heard Arnold Toynbee, the famous historian, on a television panel; and in essence he said, much as he wanted to be optimistic, he was deeply troubled when he thought of the future of Africa.

It is not only that the "Ciyuga! Ciyuga!" ("Kill! Kill!") of the Simbas sounds so fearful, or that the slaying of Dr. Paul Carlson and all the other missionaries was the worst thing that ever happened in history — for the white man has been murdering and mutilating Negroes in that unhappy land for a long time.

It is that Paul Carlson in his martyrdom symbolizes something awfully grim; and may well be a prediction of what we may expect on the Dark Continent in the days ahead.

In Africa, as *Time* magazine once pointed out, those new-born nations are but a pretense, at least in most cases. It isn't only that the untutored, drink-and-drug-crazed black men did what they did — for they were mostly tools in the hands of more intellectual and cruel men. But the sad fact is that almost all the African "nations" supported this bestial outrage on men who had come to offer the jungle men the scientific and spiritual help which was theirs to give.

Paul Carlson's medical mission at Wassolo was an emblem of the Christian spirit since Calvary that has marched through the world. And his murder is a symbol of the anti-Christ forces that have ever hurled themselves senselessly against the mercies of Christ.

The spirit of hell has enlarged itself about the earth under the spurrings of communism. Both the black and yellow races are being fired to destroy the white man by the propaganda of the Marxists in Asia and Africa. We may well yet see, as some men have predicted, an all-out world struggle between the races.

Jesus predicted this explosion of persecution against God's people. "Then shall they deliver you up to be afflicted, and shall kill you; and ye shall be hated of all nations for my name's sake."[1]

Persecutions against Christians are breaking out globally. The Scriptures predict that these persecutions will grow worse and worse until anti-Christ reigns over mankind, He who, according to Paul, shall sit in the temple of God, "showing himself that he is God."[2] Anti-Christ shall have a triple-power reign: politically, economically and religiously. "And he opened his mouth in blasphemy against God, to blaspheme his name . . . . And it was given unto him to make war with the saints, and to overcome them: and power was given him over all kindreds, and tongues, and nations. And all that dwell upon the earth shall worship him, whose names are not written in the book of life of the Lamb slain from the foundation of the world."[3]

The very Paul Carlson who fell a martyr to his faith in the tormented Congo once said, "In this century, more people have died for their witness for Christ than died in the early centuries, which we think of as the days of the martyrs."

This, of course, is true. But even at that, doubtless those who are dying at present for Him will seem small in number compared to those who must yet die for Him.

Even as we write these words a news report states that there is a rumor in Washington that we may ask for a negotiated peace in South Viet Nam. Many experts say that if this happens it may be the beginning of the surrender of all Southeast Asia to communism.

Not long ago I asked a group of people to pray for the million and a half Roman Catholics in South Viet Nam — after a CBS newscast told how the priests of that church were instructing their people how to live for God when the communists take over! We feel the day is fast approaching when *both* Catholics and Protestants shall suffer for the Lord. They shall die together, as they died together in the Congo under rebel gunfire and torture. For anti-Christ shows no favorites to any who name the name of Jesus Christ!

It is quite possible that there will be a future alliance of Catholic and Protestant churches in some sort of an ecumenical setup. But all true believers in both groups will be the ones who feel the blows of persecution from anti-Christ. The organized church may well escape some persecution — if it decided to compromise with the unchristian world — but men who take their stand for Christ shall not escape getting hurt.

Along with this over-all world picture of the revolt against Christ, we also have a revolt against Him in our own land.

This has naturally led to an explosion of crime and

violence in this country. Men who do not respect God will not respect the ordinances of men.

At Brandeis University a crowd of lawyers, sociologists, psychologists and law-enforcement officials gathered to examine and discuss the problem of violence in America. They even talked of creating a "domestic peace corps" to operate in the slum areas. They suggested that business might be brought into units to help maintain law and order. They discussed the setting up of more and newer electronic equipment to help hurry police officers to scenes of crimes. They were all agreed that violence had become so alarming in American life that something must be done, drastically and quickly.

One thing, of course, they did not discuss: they did not face the fact of *sin!*

Crisis after crisis is stacked up in this land of ours — to which the Pilgrims came in quest of freedom and justice. Anyone can glance around and see what sort of condition we are in. Hoodlums prowl through our streets in this explosion of violence until neither male nor female is safe by night, and scarcely so by day. Apostate religious leaders mouth their unbelief and cynicism in best-sellers. A clergyman stands before a school of girls and tells them how much "fun" sex is — even without marriage! Our high school girls become pregnant at an alarming, if not disgusting, rate. Vandals make our property unsafe. Robbing churches seems to have become a new game for hoodlums.

Many of our television shows evidently are beamed to morons — or toward further corrupting youth with criminal dramas. (Experts say such shows *are* affecting the kids' minds, influencing them toward crime.) The newstands are crammed with sick books awaiting their sick readers.

Yet we recently heard a church chief say: "If the world isn't getting better, God is a failure!"

An exploding world!

Nuclear explosions. Population explosion. Political explosions. Explosions of hate and persecution against the people of God.

Sometimes it might seem that the whole earth is straining toward the breaking point, like a balloon filled with gas and about to burst.

T. S. Eliot may have been quite wrong when he said the world would end in a whimper instead of a bang!

Still, despite our world conditions, our terrifying situations, with unreasonable hardheadedness man continues on his way away from the one thing that might avert him from the abyss into which he is sliding!

Ask the young fellow who came from a home where the light of Christ shone brightly; who has entered a secularistic school where the professors seem to take a sadistic delight in torturing a young man's faith! Some professors, true, do not attack religion; they pass it up with a silent sneer! The poor Christian student is pitied for his naive faith in the faith of his fathers. He might as well be a Christian in Nero's time, expecting Caesar to hear his witness for his Lord!

Well does the warning of the Apostle Paul to an earlier generation of believers apply to young Christians in our exploding era — "Be on guard; do not let your minds be captured by hollow and delusive speculations, based on traditions of man-made teaching and centered on the elemental spirits of the world and not of Christ."[4]

We speak of building a "great society"; but we may be

deceiving ourselves. David Lawrence has suggested that what we need is a "safe society" rather than a "great" one. Why do we not talk of building a *good* society, or a *Christian* society? We may well be building a monstrous tower of Babel. You cannot build a house on sand and expect it to stand — no matter how impressive the blue-prints or how costly the superstructure.

With a world exploding about us into chaos, we are pleasure-seekers instead of God-seekers. One wonders if those 200,000 dope addicts in New York City alone are but trying to *forget* what sort of a world they happen to be in! One wonders if all the alcoholics are trying to escape from facing such a human predicament as ours!

Like Rome, whose legions were scattered through the world, who tried to forget her problems and troubles and boredom through wine and carnal pleasures, do we, with our armies and navies spread abroad upon the earth and sea, seek oblivion from our responsibilities in the same way? We know how Rome ended. Have you never shuddered, wondering how the end will be in America?

3. THE TIME OF LAWLESSNESS

We seem threatened in our day with a condition bordering on anarchy. The fact is we have had sporadic anarchy in the streets in some of our cities.

In 1963, four serious crimes were committed every minute. A murder was committed every hour. There was a forcible rape attempt every half hour, and an assault every four minutes!

For every one thousand persons in our larger cities in the U.S., forty-two were arrested. Around eight hundred million dollars worth of property was stolen during the year. Since 1958, according to the FBI, the population increased eight per cent while crime increased forty per cent. Since 1960 nearly two hundred policemen have been killed defending the law. Crime cost forty-one billion last year. There were nearly 250,000 serious crimes during the year.

J Edgar Hoover who heads the FBI has spoken out against what he terms as excessive leniency which tends "to

ignore the victim and obscure the right of a free society protection under the law."

The chairman of the International Chiefs of Police appeared on a national TV panel show. After he had expressed
alarm over the fearful rise in the crime rate a newspaper
woman asked him pointedly if man's diminished fear of
hell had contibuted to this condition. The chief said he
thought so! One thought of the word of an old prophet:
"Thou hast forgotten the law of thy God."[1] When men do
not stand in awe of a divine law they may well not respect
a human law.

"Where law ends, tyranny begins," said William Pitt.
There can be no government without law, no true human
society without order. A land without a law would lie in
the hands of mobocracy.

"The law is the last result of human wisdom acting
upon human experience for the benefit of the public," said
Samuel Johnson. And, ideally, this is so. However, Rousseau
rightly said, "Good laws lead to the making of better
laws; bad ones bring about worse. As soon as any man
says of the State, 'What does it matter?' the State may be
given up for lost."

In Alexander Pope's drama Eloise says to Abelard,
"Curse on all laws but those which love has made!" But
man does not always have love. Hence laws, made even
without love, must be made for outlaws. Even then, as
Aristotle has observed, "The law has no power to command
obedience."

Richard Hooker arrived at truth when he said long
ago: "Of law there can be no less acknowledged than that
her seat is in the bosom of God." There is a Book that will
bear him out on that. All right law is from God, according
to the Scriptures. And that law is based on love. An

impressive sentence appears in the Book of Deuteronomy: "From his right hand went a fiery law for them. Yea, he loved the people!"[2]

"A law shall proceed from me, and I will make my judgment to rest for a light to the people."[3] The Law of the Almighty is given not only to condemn outlaws, but to protect law-abiding men.

A long-ago prophet lamented, "Under mine eyes outrage and injury go on, till strife is stirred and faction; and so Law is benumbed, justice is never in action — for evil men hamper the just, till justice goes awry."[4] And in our time the *Reader's Digest* ran a piece decrying the way officers of the law are handcuffed by laxity in court rulings, and the path of the criminal made easier.

Indeed the news told us of a man who shot and wounded a prowler one night in New York State. The man who was protecting his home and family faced trial and a sentence with a maximum of fourteen years — while the prowler, if found guilty, could not have gotten more than sixty days in jail.

Said J. Edgar Hoover of the FBI, "We are faced today with one of the most disturbing trends I have witnessed in my years of law enforcement: an over-zealous pity for the criminal and equivalent disregard for the victim."

The condition portrayed by Mr. Hoover tends toward more and more lawlessness. Hoods become more and more confident. Decent citizens become more and more fearful of being outraged, and the police are hampered from doing their duty.

Once criminals at least did most of their work under cover. Now they grow bolder and bolder in their grim business. Last summer we were in a Christian camp in a quiet section of Ohio, and were raided by a band of young hooligans! They even threatened to dynamite the camp because the camp president remonstrated with them.

During that same camp two boys and a girl, after singing a gospel trio number, drove homeward and stopped at a hamburger drive-in, and hooligans dragged the girl out of the car and attempted to attack her before twenty cars, occupied by people, parked at the drive-in! The two Christian boys tried to defend the girl and were slashed with switch-blades and beaten with chains!

Perhaps you read of the man in Washington who killed his wife and drove her body to a city dump and hid her there. He reported his wife as missing to the police, but they finally arrested him on suspicion of murder. He told them he had killed his wife and took them to the place where the body was hidden. He was convicted — but his conviction was reversed by the Court of Appeals. Why? Because he had made his confession without having counsel, and while in jail before he was arraigned!

Lawlessness is also aggravated greatly by the fear of involvement on the part of decent people. Social workers will tell you how people are stabbed, raped, mauled, robbed and onlookers remain aloof from it all because they are afraid of reprisals from the culprits. Witnesses to crimes are likewise afraid to testify in court. In some cases it is extremely difficult to get a jury of twelve that is not uneasy at the prospect of finding some powerful criminal guilty; they are troubled over what recriminations might follow.

Besides fear there is an appalling amount of indifference in some persons toward their fellowmen's condition. A narcotics agent was shot in a certain neighborhood. People went to their doors, but none went out to investigate. When officers asked why they had acted thus some replied that they had been watching *The Untouchables* on television and they had wanted to see how the show ended!

So lawlessness rages like a plain's fire through our streets, made worse by people's fears and indifference, and by handicaps tossed in the way of the police.

We are playing a dangerous game in our present world, a world that seems so far removed from the generation that went before us. Each seems to be trying to live apart from the rest of mankind, attempting to escape involvement in the disturbing human situation. But this way lies in monumental failure. For we *are* involved whether we like it or not. If we will not try to save others, finally we cannot save ourselves.

We fall under the deadly old despotism of looking-out-for-number-one! It is a grim trap. Forsaking the principles of God as to our responsibilities to our neighbors we wind up in a worse predicament than that of those we refused to help. Free to free others, and declining to do so, we wind up as slaves of evil dictatorships. "Men must be governed by God or they will be ruled by tyrants," said William Penn a long time ago.

We come thus to the high point of the whole dreadful matter: lawlessness is a spirit, the spirit of rebellion, not just against the laws of men, but against the very order of God. Lawlessness is the fruit of godlessness. The law-violator is a guerrilla fighting, not so much against a human government, but against the throne of the Almighty. Criminality is treason against the Creator. If law-violators seem to war only against men it is because they cannot reach God; were He accessible to them they would try to cut Him down. What is prophetic Armageddon but a massive move of men, under Satan's leadership, against the God they have warred against for ages?

We speak of God's government; but all governments, after all, are ordained of God. Even wrong governments exist by His permissive will. "He changes epochs and eras, he removes kings and he sets up kings."[5] Jesus recognized the right of Caesar to command his realm.[6] Paul wrote to the Romans: "Every Christian ought to obey the civil authorities, for all legitimate authority is derived from God's authority, and the existing authority is appointed under God. To oppose authority then is to oppose God, and such opposition is bound to be punished.

"The honest citizen has no need to fear the keepers of law and order, but the dishonest man will always be nervous of them. If you want to avoid this anxiety just lead a law-abiding life, and all that can come your way is a word of approval. The officer is God's servant for your protection. But if you are leading a wicked life you have reason to be alarmed. The 'power of the law' which is vested in every legitimate officer is no empty phrase. He is, in fact, divinely appointed to inflict God's punishment upon evil-doers.

"You should, therefore, obey the authorities, not simply because it is the safest, but because it is the right thing to do. It is right, too, for you to pay taxes for the civil authorities are appointed by God for the good purpose of public order and well-being. Give everyone his legitimate due, whether it be rates, or taxes, or reverence, or respect!"[7]

In his first epistle Peter says, "Obey every man-made authority for the Lord's sake — whether it is the emperor, as the supreme ruler, or the governors whom he has appointed to punish evildoers and reward those who do good service. It is the will of God that you may thus silence the ill-informed criticisms of the foolish. As free men you should never use your freedom as an excuse for doing something that is wrong, for you are at all times the servants of God. You should have respect for everyone; you should love our brotherhood, fear God and honor the emperor."[8]

God demands *order*, whatever kind of rulers are used to bring it about! Moreover, all the evil in a country may not, according to the Scriptures, be charged completely to the rulers. There may be more truth than many are willing to admit in the words of the old maxim-maker: "Remove scoundrels from a king, and his throne will rest on justice . . . . Many a mishap crime brings on a country: good order is maintained by honest men."[9]

Lawlessness finds no support in Sacred Writ. True, "we ought to obey God rather than men."[10] But this is only when the demands of men utterly contradict a believer's duty toward God. It is, after all, the same Peter who uttered these words in Acts that commands his fellow-Christians to obey laws and honor rulers!

Civil disobedience, as a rule, is not a Christian principle. Rioting and looting and burning are utterly condemned by the Scriptures. God ordained laws and governments and He demands decency and order. The tidal wave of lawlessness rolling through the world today is in opposition to His will. To be sure there are countless wrongs in our time, as there have been in every time; but more wrongs will not make one single wrong right.

Pandering to wrong-doing of any sort is not of the Lord. Exonerating criminals because of sentimental sympathy is not Christian. The constant attempt to find sinful men "sick" and thus make excuses for their crimes is contrary to the Bible. Sin is *never overlooked* in the Bible. It may be forgiven — even then there may be some penalty involved — but it is never excused. Even forgiveness is not granted without a plea of guilty, with no attending arguments springing from self-pity allowed.

Remember the soldier in Tolstoy's novel, *War And Peace*, who prayed, "Lord, Thou knowest I have committed many sins, but Thou also knowest I had many excellent reasons!" But the lawless soul, regardless of his "reasons," and whatever the "cause" he represents, can find no refuge in the Scriptures. They stand forever, stern and unbending, against all unlawful actions of men.

"The power of the law . . . is no empty phrase," said Paul. Oliver Wendell Holmes, Jr., has written: "The Law, wherein, as a magic mirror, we see reflected not only our own lives, but the lives of all men who have ever been! When I think of this majestic theme, my eyes dazzle!"

Much of the attitude toward law in our time might be reflected in Houseman's cynicism:

> Let God and man decree
> Laws for themselves and not for me.

But God's sovereignty is still undisputed. The words of the little rebels are pond waves beating against Gibraltar. The Law remains. The stars marching endlessly on galactic night are shouting neon-signs that the Almighty is Author of Law and Order, and His awful invisible legions of power enforce them.

"Think not that I am come to destroy the law," said Jesus.[11] That was something that even He could not do! It is high time we humble our hearts and repeat with reverence the words of the ancient poet: "The works of His hands are verity and judgment; all his commandments are sure. They stand fast for ever and ever, and are done in truth and uprightness."[12]

We can, of course, argue, with Aristotle, that the law has no power to command obedience. Someone has said,

"There is no law to make me love a man!" True; but that does not *cancel* the law! It still stands: "Thou *shalt* love thy neighbor." Granted that laws may be broken, they are not thereby *altered*. They remain. And the penalty involved in their violation remains.

Comes the question then: What are we going to do about the law? There it is; men do not always keep it. Now what?

This question may be met in several ways. The Bible meets it — but not in a way many people do. One way to meet it is by simply *changing the law to fit our misdeeds*. However, the law is God's, and the changes we make are illegal. The law stands in God's Book, unalterable, irrevocable, eternal. All our revisions are unconstitutional!

Let us proceed, next, to observe how men attempt to alter the Order of the Almighty, and with what sad results.

4. THE NEW MORALITY

Perhaps this "new morality" idea of our present period got a good start when we decided sin wasn't too sinful — and we rejected the idea of original sin altogether.

We started believing that man was naturally rational and good. We put a new trust in the State. Then Karl Marx got into the act — and anybody can see what happened next!

We had the Social Gospel, a sort of mixture between Hegelian philosophy and Fabian socialism. Then came Social Action — a mixture of existentialism and Marxism.

Existence, said the existentialist, is what matters, not essence. Don't spend too much time thinking; make choices. Life is pretty crazy, anyhow; history is rather meaningless, and about the only significance is found in personal experience.

Existentialists are divided into two camps — atheistic and theistic. The theistic one is in the church. I remember one of them saying that life is pretty ridiculous, after all; that God never grants anyone any special favors; that history has no actual moral meaning; it is unprovable that God will finally stand by His "moral law."

But you can't get rid of faith in a moral order in the universe without something happening to your morals.

If there is no moral meaning in history — where are we? If God isn't working in history, then about all we can do is set up some sort of a dictatorship to insure that we shall have what we dub "social justice." And communism likes that idea just fine!

Not only are the social and political aspects of this thing to be considered; honesty in business, integrity in industry, and many other items are involved. What about individual liberty, and property rights? After all, who needs "rights" in a universe that is morally meaningless? Power is what matters. And more power — like Nietzsche said some time back. With a society that finds no footprints of God in human history, what can happen but a global government? That global government is predicted in the Scriptures; but its head is anti-Christ, not Christ!

In a world where morals are meaningless and God does not move in history, little wonder we prattle of the need for a "new morality." The old morals just don't fit our present-day mood. So we, rather than altering our mood, prefer to change our morals.

One of the mightiest impacts made on men by this changing attitude toward God and His world is in our sex life.

Usually sex is a fine thing to go by to see whether we are ascending or descending the moral scale, for sex we have with us always — whether we're good or bad, collectivistic or democratic, liberal or conservative. And it's always very important to us.

So come our changes regarding our views of sex. What

we seek most, apparently, is a new moral code that will easily accommodate itself to defying much of the old code comprehended in the Hebrew and Christian standards.

First we turn to the mind experts. We have a habit of turning to them these days about everything under the sun. Without the "thus saith the psychologists" we flounder in the breakers of confusion. We must approach them as devotees approached a powerful high priest in the old days, waiting for them to define, explain, and interpret.

A psychologist in Miami says that sex is not even a moral question. We should not ask, "Is it right or wrong?" he says, but "is it feasible? Will it enrich my life personally? Will it help my health?" He goes on to state that his view is fast becoming the view of many Protestant church leaders. The preachers, he says, no longer wag their fingers at the young folk because they surrender to biological urges and do some experimenting. They don't yell, "Stop! That's wrong!" Rather they ask, "Is it meaningful?"

Imagine asking a couple of impassioned kids if the sex experience was meaningful! They'd probably find the thing plenty meaningful. For the moment at least!

We need something more than questions like that to keep the kids from making fools of themselves and ruining their young lives. We need discipline, and faith, and a fear of God. We need the Cross; and we need to lay it on the line out of the Word: "The soul that sins it shall die!"

True, God thinks sex is fine. He invented it! But He also made restrictions for it which He Himself thought up. And the sex act, outside these restrictions, is a ruinous thing. Ask the young fellow who has just discovered that he has a venereal infection. Ask the young girl who finds she is going to be a mother when she has no husband. Ask them what the mouthings of the "new moralists" can do for them? We are so constituted, and we live in a world so arranged, that we cannot violate God's laws with impunity.

Some of the older psychologists warned us of the dangers involved in unrestricted sexual action. Dr. Sorokin of Harvard University warned America that sex could send the nation down the drain. Dr. Sorokin never claimed, as far as I know, to be an evangelical Christian.

Again and again we read pieces from celebrated writers, many of them not churchmen, who deplore our dreadful obsession with sex, warning us of the doom that lies ahead if we continue as we are. They are aware that no kingdom, or civilization, ever survived an obsession with sexual impurity.

A few symbols could be drawn over against the fall of any civilization or empire; and one of these would be a nude woman!

To decry feminine nakedness is, of course, like asking to be called a "bluenose." It's like protesting air conditioning during a long, hot summer! If one spends an evening at TV without seeing a near-nude female it will be an exception. Nudity is getting to be as much a novelty as hamburger stands!

Unclad females have invaded our newsstands as locusts invaded Egypt in Moses' time. One Broadway columnist cracked that "the sexiest place in town" was the Sunday magazine of a famous New York newspaper. However, we need not tarry overlong in the realm of entertainment and the press to behold the skin-exposure on a grand scale. Just take a walk down the street in the good old summertime!

Gaze among the raucous hucksters of American com-

modities and see the skin show unlimited. "Nudity is here
to stay in advertising," said a topflight account executive
of a garment firm. "Nudity is inherent in the product,"
assert the makers of a certain piece of apparel. The better
known models are stepping down into the lingerie lineup.

A few newspaper editors have deplored the spread of
nudity — such as Lloyd Jenkins Jones of Tulsa. But they
seem not to have been heard, much less heeded. "Sex is
here to stay" is a dated wisecrack. Nakedness, it appears,
is also here to stay. One burlesque theater owner lamented,
"The competition on the sidewalk is terrific!"

Mr. Khrushchev cried that the immodesty of Americans shocked him. For once he may have been telling the
truth. Americans of a generation ago would have been
shocked at our women's dresslessness. In history nakedness
and wantoness go together. Sex seems to rise up and cry
aloud in the day that sin brings down judgment on a
world. This was true before the fall of Babylon, Egypt,
Assyria and Rome.

When we discussed this with a prominent clergyman
he pointed out that the Bible has more to say about our
being overdressed than undressed. This could be a fact.
However, although you may not find in Scripture a direct
order, "Thou shalt not go naked," neither will you find an
endorsement of nudist camps.

Taken as a whole the Bible seems to look with a particular sort of loathing upon nakedness in society. Granted
the Book opens on a naked pair who were unashamed.
But they were also presented as being *innocent* — and we
are not.

Many of the prophets of Israel and Judah used nudity
as a symbol of divine judgment. Passing sentence upon
Babylon, the Lord said, "Thy nakedness shall be uncovered,

yea, thy shame shall be seen."[1] Against Nineveh sounds the warning, "I will shew the nations thy nakedness, and the kingdoms thy shame."[2] The Spirit pleads with the Laodiceans, "Buy of me . . . white raiment, that thou mayest be clothed, and that the shame of thy nakedness do not appear."[3]

A psychologist states that the undress of women often contributes to the dreadful doings of sex-maniacs. True, he said, the sex-fiend is psychotic, and if women wore clothes like Arabian women of a century ago, he would still be psychotic; yet the near-nudity of women may trigger the fiend's mania and make it more operative.

If this be true, a responsibility is involved for the Christian woman. Jesus warned men not to look upon a woman with lust. But what if the woman provokes this desire by her immodesty — shall she be guiltless?

Cleo Shupp wrote a piece for a national magazine deploring the way American mothers thrust their little daughters into situations which they should never have to meet. She asks us to observe, at a basketball game in a school gymnasium, how, when the band parades, girls, under ten, display themselves in sequinned low-cut short-short costumes, exposing themselves like chorus girls for the entertainment of fawning adults. How, asks the author, can such children ever be lured back to doll-playing, where they rightly belong? Cleo Shupp is not a preacher; she is a writer. Religion was not mentioned in her article in the *Saturday Evening Post*. But she is concerned about *decency*! And she protests against seeing indecency promoted in small females before they know what immodesty means.

One clergyman has said that a man must be inherently wrong in his spirit before he is tempted through a woman's lack of dress. But more than the spirit must be taken into account. The flesh is involved. Far too often, as Jesus observed, "The flesh is weak."

It is impossible, from a Scriptural viewpoint, to discover any support for the public exhibition of a person's body. It just isn't Christian — if we go by the Book.

In our most reverent and solemn moments we clothe ourselves, and not merely because of social mores. In the presence of the Creator and our fellowmen, we feel the need of being decently dressed. When we grow lean spiritually, and reckless morally, we throw off our clothes with our restraints.

The figure of a naked woman has been the sign of lewdness and lust from old time. The Gospel does not, in so many words, thunder against it. But there is a tone in the New Testament that utterly condemns immodesty in dress. The Scriptural denunciation of all sexual impurity does not leave our near nude way of life untouched by the judgment of God.

Having said all this, it now seems impossible that the clergy once denounced indecency of dress from the pulpit! But it is a fact.

And how are things in that direction now? Have you read Bishop John Robinson's famous book, *Honest to God*? He cites examples of men going to prostitutes, with alleged benefits in his argument that a man may go in to a whore to the glory of God! He also thinks we should not reject the homosexual.

If Bishop Robinson stood alone in this matter — as he *would* have a few years ago! — we might dismiss him as a crackpot, albeit an intellectual one. But he has many supporters. One minister has come out with the idea that premarital sex activity might be more therapeutical than iniquitous for the youngsters. It might be beneficial to their health! One clergyman in New York told his congregation that *Fanny Hill* was a moral book. (*Fanny Hill* is the autobiography of a prostitute, depicted in filthy detail!) This same minister also said that pornography is not a bad thing for people to read, anyhow! He was going to deliver a few copies of *Fanny Hill* to his parishoners, but the police stepped in and stopped him!

But to get down to business about this "new morality" — what's *new* about it?

There aren't any new morals any more than there are new sins! Try to name one crime that a man may commit today that he couldn't have committed, in one way or another, at any time in history. Murder is not modern, nor robbery, nor lying. Man once worshiped gods of mud and rock; today he worships gods of money and success. Men once sold their daughters for sexual use to men; now they swap their *wives*, for free, to other men! Slavery may have changed its name, but it is still the same thing it always was in lands ruled by brutal dictators.

Just what does this new morality consist of? Take up the old standards — let's keep this very simple. In our new code what shall we put? What shall we do? Kill? Steal? Commit libel? Grab another man's wife? Burn a neighbor's house? Get drunk and make fools of ourselves?

But, someone says, how about men and women performing the sex act, apart from marriage? (We've already discussed this, but, it's a hard theme to avoid, especially when we discuss this "new morality" thing!) Our objector says, "Why should we go to hell for doing what comes naturally?" Well, we've seen some beat-up kids, both male and female, living in some sort of hell over "doing what comes naturally." Ask the social worker, the minister, the doctors, the police. Going all-out in this sex business is *not* good for anyone in *this life*, even if we ignore the judgment of the life to come.

Just what is this "new morality" supposed to *do* for us, anyhow?

What's wrong with us? Why must we try to change the laws of God and good men for worse laws? Why don't we return to those old, tried laws and go by them instead of dreaming up new ones that are meaningless as well as hurtful to us all? How sin blinds the world.

The "new morality" is not new.

It's the *old immorality!*

5. THE TRUTH-CHANGERS

In this time of lawlessness, and the "new morality" what we face is the fact that men, in the name of "progress," or "pragmatism," or "existentialism," are trying, in the words of Paul, to "change the truth of God into a lie."[1]

The New Testament has a classic example of how an addendum to the Word may have sad consequences. Jesus said in His Sermon on the Mount, "Ye have heard that it hath been said, Thou shalt love thy neighbor, and hate thine enemy."[2] The first part of that sentence is Scriptural. Moses did indeed order the people to love their neighbors. But one looks in vain for the last half of that sentence in Israel's law! When did God tell us to hate our enemies? Some misguided earthling added that last clause. Jesus didn't say it was in the Bible; He said, "Ye have *heard* that it hath been said." A moment's reflection will reveal the fallacy of that clause. It might just happen that a man's *foe* was his next-door neighbor!

What damage this added clause does to the original commandment, "Love thy neighbor." How easily we make a foe out of a friend, then have a reason to hate him! An altered truth, like a half-truth, is always a dangerous thing.

Man possesses an ingenuity for error — the ability to convert God's message into a devilish doctrine. How often a few pen strokes change a shining truth into a dark lie!

Satan started this business of truth-changing long ago. He corrupted an order from heaven by a single three-letter word. God had said that if Adam violated a certain rule he would die. But the devil said, "You shall *not* surely die." Such a short word — and the future of the race bound up with it! One tiny word inserted into God's order — and "death passed upon all men."

With what shallow reasoning, and how glibly we change the truth! We say, "Oh, it doesn't mean *that*!" Or we say, "Somehow, I just can't accept that." Once a lady poet cried, in a moment of ecstasy, "I accept the universe!" To which thick-skinned Thomas Carlyle snorted, "She'd better!" Just so. And we'd better accept God's eternal truth — if we want to live!

Jesus came and told us that we must repent of our sins. We must be changed. We must be born from above. Paul said that we must be new creatures. Something must happen to us — something that only God can do. But along comes a man who says, "The kingdom of God is within you. That's in the Bible!" He uses Scripture to show that we are *already* right, without a new birth. By a clever shuffling of messages in the Book, putting one truth over against another, he changes the truth into a lie!

I met a man who denied that God ever made contact with guilty men. He dug up a Scripture verse to prove it — "We know that God heareth not sinners."[3] It's true if we fence that verse away from the rest of the Word that God will pay no attention whatever to anyone who ever violated

His Law. But how shall any man, then, be saved, seeing we have all sinned and come short of the glory of God? How wrong to tear a text from its context and build a temple on it! The men who said, "God hears not sinners" were themselves sinners — although they would never have admitted it! The Pharisees made that statement after they had consulted a blind man whom Jesus healed. They simply didn't know what they were talking about! God *does* hear sinners. He hears them, and saves them.

This truth-altering is the most dangerous game man ever played. In almost the same breath in which Paul states that men change the truth into a lie he says that they change "the glory of the uncorruptible God into an image made like to corruptible man."[4] How busy man is, making "images" that suit his fancy better than the One who is the Creator of all things! Men who will change the truth of God will also exchange God Himself for another god. To alter the Truth is an attempt to alter the God who gave the Truth. Tampering with the Almighty! It's dangerous — but men do it.

Actually, though, man never changes the truth into a lie! He cannot accomplish this feat any more than he can actually change God. Nothing changes God's truth. It remains forever the same, from age unto age. What happens is that a man does turn the truth into a lie for *himself!* To him who changes it, it becomes a trap, a thing of doom. Paul intimates in another place that truth, rejected, tampered with, turns out to be a "strong delusion" which leads to damnation.[5]

Jesus said, "I am the Truth." Who could change *Him?* But see how, through the tormented ages of human history. men have striven to change Him! They make Him a mere man. They strip away His glory and His authority and put

Him on a level with wretched, fallen mankind. They smile behind their hands at mention of His miracles. They put Him in the grave at last — and leave Him there! For them, He never cracks the tomb, never ascends to His Father, shining and triumphant!

Judgment follows judgment because we do this to Him. He tells us that if we take the sword we shall perish by the sword. We don't believe Him. We make Him mean something else. But see how the sword glitters and whistles toward us! He tells us that unless we repent we shall perish. We shrug at that; repentance is an old-fashioned word unfit for sophisticated people. Meantime, we tremble lest the atom-gale should blow and take us all away!

Let's not make the picture all dark. Some men *accept* the Truth. They rejoice in it. They love it. They would not alter it one whit, rather will they change their lives to live by it. They know that nothing that has ever happened, or will ever happen, can make the Truth of no effect.

They see all Truth mirrored in Him "who came forth from the Father, and came into the world." He is forever changeless. He is eternally right about things. He is God come to man; and "it is impossible for God to lie."[6]

To some of us, Christ is utterly perfect — just as He is! We need no "new morality" to improve His way. We accept His Gospel — as it is. It thrills us, just as He gave it. In keeping with Jesus' immortal promise some men have found the Truth, and the Truth makes them free.

6. THE WAY TO 'NOTHINGARIANISM'

Lawlessness is enchanced, the "new morality" supported by our modern method of scrapping great theology, sneering at old creeds, laughing off old fundamentals of the faith. We are caught in a maelstrom of religious nihilism.

Newsweek reported that many students at Stanford University considered the religion on the campus as a sort of Anythingarianism. ("Anythingarians" was what Jonathan Swift dubbed those religionists who were so "broad-minded" that they were empty of spirit.)

It seems rather odd to observe modern day students asking for a better brand of religion on a college campus. The college authorities told them that if they were not satisfied with the Memorial Church they could attend downtown churches of their choice. Students complained, however, that the downtown churches offered little relevant to the needs of youth. They just didn't respond, said the students, to the young people's curiosity about religion.

One need not visit a university campus these days to bump into some Anythingarians. They are all about.

47

Asking many men today about what they really believe might be like asking a four-year-old about abiogenesis.

Alexander Pope might have been speaking to our time when he said people attended church "not for the doctrine, but for the music." (And some would rather their music wasn't too theologically inclined!) Artemas Ward might form a goodly fellowship out of those, like him, who find their religion of an exceeding accommodating character.

One poet said:
What if men take to following where He leads
Weary of mumbling Athanasian creeds?

But does history report many committed Christians who scrapped their creeds? Lizette Reese quipped:

Creeds grow so thick along the way,
Their boughs hide God.

But a creedless religion might do even a better job of hiding Him.

I once saw a sign on a temple: "No Creed But Christ." Well, that's a fair-sized creed if you ask me! Jesus warned His disciples against accepting "just anything" theologically. "He bade them beware . . . of the doctrine of the Pharisees and Saducees."[1] He knew the danger of teaching an ethical life without giving men an adequate theology. "The people were astonished at his doctrine, for he taught them as one having authority, and not as the scribes."[2] His theology came from an Authority forever changeless. "My doctrine is not mine, but his that sent me."[3]

Anythingarianism is not only ineffective for Christian character and performance; it is dangerous. It may even be diabolical. Paul refers to the "doctrine of devils."[4] Men seduced by such doctrines are men who "depart from the faith." Without foundational doctrines how shall we know whether our ideas are from God or Satan? The man in the pulpit, Paul warned Timothy, should be "a good minister of Jesus Christ, nourished up in the words of faith and of good doctrine."[5] Bishops were not to depend entirely on living excellent lives; they must also be found "holding fast the faithful Word" in order to be "able by sound doctrine both to exhort and to convince the gainsayers." We are not asked to adorn proper deportment with proper dogma; we are required to adorn the doctrine with good works. Doctrine is basic; it is the foundation.

Anythingarianism is a theological tragedy. Ages ago a prophet said that to "utter error" was "to make empty the soul of the hungry."[6] A New Testament scribe warned: "Be not carried about with divers and strange doctrines."[7] Those primitive believers were afraid of Anythingarianism!

One might easily by-pass the brief missive in the New Testament known as Second John. But it contains an impressive admonition. The writer urges believers to remember that the "good life" does not comprehend the full credentials of a Christian. Theology and dogma must be involved. "Anyone who . . . does not stand by the doctrine of Christ is without God; he who stands by the doctrine possesses both the Father and the Son." But John does not stop at this point — and how quickly he would be dubbed an "extremist" or a "bigot" in our time of believe-whatever-you-please! John hurls his "narrow-minded" charge: "If anyone comes to you who does not bring this doctrine, do not welcome him into your house or give him a greeting." (N.E.B.). What a non-conformist! But John is not finished. "Anyone who gives him a greeting is an accomplice of his wicked deed!"

Anythingarianism finds no support in the New Testament. Nor has it built enduring temples along the theological road of history. Does it matter what a person believes? Ask Joseph in Potiphar's house. Ask Paul in his Roman prison. Ask John Huss on his way to the fire. Men *are* what they believe.

The man who does not know what he believes may too soon believe in nothing. Anythingarianism is the road to "Nothingarianism"! It is the way to theological nihilism; but it is more. It is the end of the road for faith itself. For faith without a theology is not only dead; it is impossible.

7. THE ENEMY OF THE FAITH

We are apt to overlook an important fact in our discussion of present-day disrespect for the principles of righteousness. That is: man is aided and abetted in his lawlessness by a powerful and slaughterous foe! A famous Scotch theologian has said that such an enemy must exist, for man is incapable of doing all the wrongs he does on his own; he has to have some outside help.

So we must consider the devil.

Did you read about what happened to five-year-old Larry? He was beaten for twenty or thirty minutes at a time by foster parents. They beat him with a three-foot length of rubber molding, with a stick two feet long and an inch thick, and with their hands and fists until he died. The coroner stood appalled at the bruises and marks on the lifeless little body.

That happened in Indianapolis. Day afer day we read reports such as this in the press. And we hear how Hitler and Eichmann murdered millions of Jews. We discover that the Chinese communists liquidated *twenty million* people

51

who stood in their way to conquest of China. We are shocked at the atrocities committed all over the earth and in all history.

We approach the authorities about such matters, and the experts, and ask the reason for man's inhumanity to man; and we may be told that these brutal souls are sick. They had unhappy childhoods. They are troubled with long-ago traumas. Somewhere, someone threw a monkey wrench into their mental machinery, or "fouled up" their emotional apparatus. They are victims of the past rather than criminals in the present.

But some of us, like the Scotch theologian, think these folk may have had outside help.

The devil shows up very early in the Bible, appearing several times in the Old Testament. In the New Testament Jesus scarcely comes to His ministry before Satan appears to oppose Him. All through the Book we find ourselves constantly running into devils. J. S. Whale has reminded us that Paul mentions the devil in every one of his letters but Philemon.

In various translations of the Bible we have different names for these enemies that indwell men. They are mostly referred to as "spirits." They are designated as "evil," "unclean" and "foul." Never does the Bible have anything favorable to say about them.

The New Testament gives us glimpses of demon characteristics. Demons appear quite aware of God's existence, so much so that they are disturbed![1] The certainty of the judgment brings them terror.[2] They recognize Jesus as God's Son.[3] They recognize those who hold high positions in God's Kingdom.[4] They are represented as speaking in their own person.[5] Jesus connects demon possession with the power of Satan.[6]

The Scriptures reveal something of demoniac action on human personality. Demons produce irreverence toward God.[7] They make men spiritually hopeless,[8] urge them into violence,[9] seduce them from the faith,[10] afflict them physically.[11]

Demoniac power enabled one girl to be a fortune-teller.[12] Demons were operative among the spiritiually-minded.[13] They troubled children as well as adults.[14] It was possible to be possessed by more than one demon.[15]

At this point, of course, it is time to page Dr. Bultmann, or someone, for a fast job of demythologizing! Nobody believes in demons any more. We have aberrations, dementia, traumas, phobias and alcoholism; we have disturbed emotions and complexes; but you hardly ever run into a demon these days. Demons have been exorcised, along with the goblins and ghosts.

Jesus, however, was "naive" enough to believe in demons. Apparently He had no difficulty whatever in accepting them as a fact. He never bothered to explain anything about them, or show clearly their operative processes; He simply ousted them from folk. When he met a frothy-mouthed man in Gadara, naked, wild-eyed and dangerous, He didn't suggest that the fellow be committed to an institution for shock treatment. Evidently He was assured that the fellow was demon-possessed. He might have appeared rather ridiculous ordering a trauma or aberration of the mind from the troubled Gadarene into a herd of hogs!

And when a woman came to Him stating that her daughter had a devil, He didn't say, "Lady, let's not be naive. Devils don't exist. Your daughter has some difficulty yes; but a good psychiatrist could do her a world of good. Whatever her affliction is, rest assured that she is not possessed of devils!" If Jesus questioned the mother's diagnosis of her child's trouble, He was quite silent about it.

When the Master discovered His disciples trying to oust a demon from a man, He did not reprimand them with: "Men, if you're going to meet the world as an inteligent group you'll have to forget about satanic entities indwelling human personalities. Such things won't stand up before the test-tube and the slide rule. You'll have folk laughing themselves sick at you. This fellow obviously has something wrong with him. Restore him, of course, if you can — but don't let people hear you talking about demons. They'll advise *you* to consult a psychiatrist."

The Apostle Paul, for all his ability to think, also believed in these devilish entities. I heard a minister say to his congregation, "Paul spoke of wrestling with principalities in high places. Evidently the apostle accepted the common error of his day — the existence of demons. Since we now know that demons are nonexistent we assume Paul was referring to man's bent toward evil." The clergyman didn't explain how he knew demons were nonexistent, or what it was that bent man so inexorably toward evil.

Some time ago there appeared in *Christian Life* an article by a clergyman who had been an alcoholic. He told of his struggles over his defection; but it was only when he came to see he was possessed of a devil that he prayed for deliverance from the foe. God responded to his prayer and freed him from his bondage.

Who dares to stand outside this man's life, not having known the tormenting trials or the deep, dark mysterious combat within him, and say that the man was mistaken about discovering a demon in his life? It is utterly impossible to prove scientifically that the man was *not* demon-possessed. The man himself was convinced about the demon.

And, watching Jesus work in the New Testament story, how can we doubt but what *He* would have agreed with the minister's self-diagnosis?

Surely we live in an age of paradox. We have gotten rid of the devil; we have eliminated all demons. Yet what deviltry goes on in our world! How many demons bob up in our daily newscasts!

Evil is a towering mystery. Sin is a vast dark riddle. We have never been able to tell what gives a man his stubborn bent toward wrongness, his awful drive toward darkness. Because evil is mysterious shall we deny it as a fact? Likewise with demons: because we can't penetrate their dark nature shall we write them off as figments of the human imagination? Because we have not discovered a demon under the microscope shall we say he is a myth?

Some of us go along with the Man from Nazareth. He who has flooded the ages with His spiritual wisdom and disturbed us with His strange insight into our own nature, as well as His knowledge of God, must not be shrugged off at any point. Amazing as it sounds when He says, "Come unto me, all ye that labor and are heavy-laden, and I will give you rest," still we believe Him, and go to Him. Incredible as is His calm statement, "Before Abraham was, I am," we bow our heads in the affirmative. Mind-staggering as is His announcement, "He that hath seen me, hath seen the Father," we cry, "My Lord, and my God!"

So with demons! He believed in them. He accepted them as real. Shall we, at this point of mystery, wag our heads? And, having wagged our heads, shall we say we have rejected His position because we are logical and scientific?

I keep thinking of a coroner who examined the body of a small girl who had been chained, starved and beaten by her parents until she died. The coroner said, "Can this be the work of human beings? It must be the work of devils!" We might imagine Jesus nodding solemnly at the coroner, saying, "When you pray say, 'Our Father, deliver us from the evil one!'"

We should remember that while lawless forces sweep through the world like a gale, men are mutinous not only against the laws of earth but against the laws of heaven. It is a stepping up, as we move toward the reign of anti-Christ, of the rebellion Satan has long carried on against his Enemy.

We, as mere mortals, are incapable of meeting such a murderous opponent without divine help. Only the Cross and the Spirit and the Word can sustain us when the red-hot powers of hell assault all the bastions of right and decency. Men have always needed God, but in our day we seem to need Him in a special sense.

8. THE FORGOTTEN ANGER

It might be a good thing at this point to pause long enough to consider one other element that contributes to the insurgence of restless souls and indifference to right principles: Men have forgotten the anger of God.

We have forgotten that His wrath is mentioned more often in the Scriptures than His love. And because we have forgotten this — while we prattle on and on about His love, ignoring the fact that love is not soft and indulgent, but stern and demanding at times — we feel free to violate His rules, telling ourselves that a good God would not punish us.

A church chieftain has said that the pulpit today does not need a message of doom; such will only further alienate people from God. We need, says this clergyman, to hear how God pours out His love and His Spirit upon mankind.

But I checked through a Bible concordance regarding that word "pour," and discovered that indeed God does pour out His love and Spirit upon men; but His "pouring" in another direction reaches immense proportions.

What God is pouring out more than anything else is anger!

This, of course, jars the impassivity of the modern mind. Nobody gets angry any more, especially over such things as moral principles. Regarding the violations of the rules of righteousness, everybody is pretty calm and collected. The man who gets agitated over "sin" may find himself being gently shooed toward a psychiatrist. It's the period of adjustment, conformity and togetherness.

Wrath is especially taboo in the pulpit. An angry preacher is as welcome as a water buffalo in a chicken hatchery. So for God to be angry, naturally is out of the question. The earth-scorching indignation of the Almighty belongs to another and more unenlightened time.

Yet — glance through the Bible. Therein the wrath of God is a disturbing thing. To be sure the divine fury is not confined to the Hebrew and Christian Scriptures. The old pagans proclaimed the wrath of God, or of the gods.

Admittedly the anger of the Lord is not easily analyzed. Certainly it does not have its counterpart in the mad passions of the carnal-minded mortal. But whatever the wrath of God is, or is not, it is something to consider with awe. For He pours out His wrath like water.[1] He pours out fury as fire.[2]

Moses warns: "The anger of the Lord . . . shall smoke!" Plagues and devastation should follow disobedience to the divine order, until the land should be as Sodom. The nations would ask, "What meaneth the heat of this great anger?"[3]

In one prophetic outburst God's wrath runs to colossal proportions — "I mean to muster the nations and assemble all the realms, to vent my wrath upon them, the full heat of my anger, for the fire of my fury shall consume the whole earth."[4] Obviously, it is not a mere "scolding" that the Lord has in mind for the people.

Such passages as the preceding might cause some of our moderns to cast about for a cosmic psychiatric ward for the Almighty! To see God in this role spoils our "image" of Him!

Some flee the Old Testament, where God's wrath smokes often, seeking in the New Testament refuge from the angry Deity of the Hebrew prophets. After all, that God back there was rather inclined to emotional disturbances; it didn't take much to trigger Him into an explosion. He was angry at things that would scarcely ruffle even our most irreverent pundit of today. God has changed — rather our view of Him has changed. He is the cosmic Gentleman. He never goes off on a tangent. He exercises decorum. And He wouldn't hurt an impenitent flea!

The New Testament refuge fails the escapee from the wrath of the Old. God's anger is evident in the gospels and the epistles. And when we come to the Apocalypse His wrath is a fearful thing to behold.

There is Jesus in the gospels — good, kind, merciful, full of empathy, sympathy and compassion. But He gets angry. He burns fiercely when the legalists torment Him with their theological stupidity. His lash sends the money-changers scrambling from the Temple.

Without Jesus' messages on retribution the preachers of an earlier generation could never have found material for their devastating sermons on hell! Bertrand Russell says that one of the major reasons why he rejected Christianity is Jesus' terrifying doctrine of the sinner's damnation! Indeed, pictures portraying Jesus looking like a docile "do-gooder" seem rather incongruous in face of His prophetic thunder — "Depart from me, ye cursed, into ever-lasting fire, prepared for the devil and his angels."[5]

The anger of God is never played down in the writings of the Apostle Paul. That anger is "revealed from heaven against all ungodliness and unrighteousness."[6] It is discovered in inexorable opposition to all who perpetrate evil.[7] Sexual impurity, even indecent conversation, bring down the Lord's wrath.[8] Men who hinder the witness of the Gospel expose themselves to the divine indignation: "The Wrath is on them to the bitter end!"[9]

In the Book of Revelation God's anger blazes perhaps more fiercely then elsewhere in the Scriptures. Our fathers found there an awesome text — "The great day of his wrath is come; and who shall be able to stand?"[10] All in all it is a rather terrifying Book — especially to unbelievers. And however we may view its imagery we never find God indulgent toward sin. Wrath rolls thunderously through its pages. He who seeks a place to hide from the theology of the heavenly anger should eschew the last book in the New Testament!

Are we justified in pursuing our theme on the anger of the Lord? We have but one reply: Are the Bible scribes right about the divine anger? *Is* God as those men insist He is? Or is He more like the God discovered in our modern thought? He can scarcely be both.

If the Scriptures present a true picture of God's wrath, then we are confronted with something more than just theological implications. There is a vast social aspect involved. We have already referred to the chairman of the International Chiefs of Police who said that our ignoring the divine retribution for sin aggravates our lawless condition today. Once we spoke of an upright man as a God-fearing individual. There is no deterrent to evil like man's awe of the Almighty.

Who can say what the results might be if the pulpits generally proclaimed the wrath of God in our world? We could never know unless we tried it. Billy Graham has been quoted as saying that he cannot expect men to come to Christ without preaching on God's judgment. And from a Scriptural viewpoint God's wrath and His judgments are forever associated.

If the wrath of God is real, then only repentance and moral recovery will turn it aside. If the anger of God is a fact we may feel its impact — too late to do much about it! We might do well to consider the words of Thomas Jefferson: "I tremble for my nation when I reflect that God is just, and that His justice never sleeps!"

A Hebrew prophet declared what the Lord did to one of the most powerful dynasties of the ancient world — "His blazing anger he let loose, fury and rage and ruin, the messengers of woe; straight and swift his anger sped, unsparing."[11] Pharaoh might have testified to that wrath; he was its target!

The anger of God is not an easy theme to take into the pulpit. A man must do it with humility and compassion. Yet how shall the gospel minister neglect it? The message belongs in the pulpit. It is relevant; it is the Word of God. It is bound up with the ordination of the prophet. The messenger of Christ is under orders to sound it; for from what is a man saved if not from "the Wrath to come"?

Precisely at this point is revealed the power and the glory of the Gospel — against this background of divine wrath and judgment. Here the Cross gleams the brightest; and grace has a heart-breaking wonder. Here, against the backdrop of thunderous Sinai, does Christ stand, significant, God-sent and calling a world to eternal life. We are moved by God's love; but we are the more deeply moved when we see that love standing between us and God's wrath.

9. THE DIAGNOSIS IS NOT ENOUGH!

At the close of the preceding chapter we have hinted at what we want to lay emphasis upon now. Heretofore we have stressed the unruliness of men, the laxity toward righteousness. We have diagnosed our situation.

But diagnosis, of course, is not enough.

After all the diagnosticians are legion! Marya Mennes had an impressive piece in *McCall's* recently called "The Thin Gray Line." She wrote of evil that often wears the mask of respectability. Refrain-like through her piece run the words: "They all do it." Cops taking small payoffs in gifts; folk padding expenses on income tax returns — things like that. Everybody does it. Nobody is willing to assume responsibility; everybody blames his defections on some-one else.

"Good" and "bad" don't exist; conscience is a word for the ancients, it's outdated. All this, of course, warns Marya Mennes, leads to ruin for our nation if the downward progress isn't checked — soon. The "They-All-Do-It" chorus is drowning the voice of ethics; we teeter on the edge of chaos.

But what to do? Marya Mennes makes an almost futile gesture toward solving our fearful problem. Maybe, she suggests, we should not worry about prayers in public schools, but teach ethics, law and individual responsibility to society. We need to fortify our conscience. Make parents attend these sessions at school. Corruption is involving us all. So ends the essay.

Pick up most any magazine — except the filthy ones with all the naked women and smart-aleck articles by wise-cracking pagans — and you may find something similar to the piece in *McCall's*. One writer deplores our making little girls behave like adults. Another writes about kids that cut auto tires and wreck nice homes. Still another laments the sexual immorality in our high schools. A famous newscaster announces that millions of Americans will steal! Police chiefs and FBI warn that crime is increasing at a staggering rate. Multitudinous voices are crying the same sad story of our stampede to doom.

And most of the writers wind up with inadequate answers for our heart-breaking situation. Seldom do we hear any feasible suggestion to bring us back to sanity and safety.

There is also the voice of Billy Graham, and other lesser voices — voices in the wilderness, also crying the same disturbing tale of our sorrowful plight. But these voices are different in that they get down to business and, beyond diagnosis, offer an answer to our problem. *Sin*, they say, is the problem, and Christ is the answer to our sin.

They tell us that man has something terribly wrong with him. He's warped, twisted, has a bent toward evil. Sin is subtle. It makes a man captive, and he cannot do what he would, even when his judgment warns him he will destroy himself if he doesn't change. Like millions of

Americans trying to quit cigarettes, yet still smoking even when confronted by the possibility of cancer, man cannot change his ways. He needs help. He needs the grace of God. He needs the miracle that comes through a child-like faith in Christ.

The gospel men find both their diagnosis and their remedy in the Bible, but far too few people are listening to them. "Oversimplification!" snorts the pundit. The gifted writers in the big magazines keep holding out the fearful diagnosis of our condition, and the diagnosis is read by millions. One might think that since no real specific is offered by others we might at least *try* that offered by the gospel men!

These evangels can present cases of impressive cures, testimonies from those healed of sin. History reports vast numbers of such. The Acts of the Apostles is a mighty chronicle of men redeemed by grace. Seeing that our evangels offer *something* you would think that millions should be willing to consider their message. Yet many of the same scribes who have diagnosed our condition so ably, might be the first to scoff at the remedy offered by spiritually-minded men, calling them "crackpots" and their message "irrelevant."

Most of the magazines, if not all, which published the diagnosis and paid good money for such, would scarcely publish a piece on the New Birth, which Jesus said every man must have to see the kingdom of God. The truth is that some *religious* magazines will not publish pieces that set forth unflinchingly the demands of the New Testament.

More articles will run in our magazines deploring our dangerous situation, our lack of morals, our irresponsibilities, our flagging conscience. How far must we hang over the cliff before we ask the Bible about the redemptive message? Or will we *ever* ask? We dig in the ashes of nations that didn't ask, marveling that so much grandeur and glory came to dust. Is this to be our fate also?

Still, our evangels hold out the positive hope for our ills, both orally and in print. In the midst of spreading darkness the Light still blazes and the darkness cannot put it out. Centuries ago Jesus warned, "Iniquity shall abound," and our situation proves the truth of His prophecy. But Jesus also promised that the Gospel of the Kingdom should be preached to all nations. Whether the world will accept this witness or not in time to avoid ruin, the witnesses themselves are under divine orders to lift the Cross against the night, even to the end of the age. Thus Jesus not only proves He is a true Prophet, but bears a Redeemer's love for mankind, and that even for such a sin-sick world as ours His mercy and patience are immeasurable.

As Jesus promised, His messengers will continue to hold out the one effective answer to our illness; and this, in the over-all view of history, will be more important than any ideas of philosophy or discoveries of science. The prophets in the wilderness may, like the long-ago Baptist be rejected; but in the message is the ring of eternal trumpets.

10. THE WAY OUT

In our time of insurgence and disorder which often borders on anarchy, in this hour of immorality and indecency, as we have said, diagnosis of the situation is not enough. Even law enforcement is not enough — for law enforcement, if it reaches certain proportions, might result in tyranny.

The law itself cannot make men right in their hearts. Thomas Carlyle once told his mother that if he should go into the pulpit to preach he would say, "You people know what to do, so go out and do it!" His Scotch mother wiser in spiritual matters than her famous son, said, "Aye, Thomas — but will you also tell them *how* to do it?"

The law cannot make men right. No law keeps me from burning my neighbor's house. I may be jailed for it — but the house will still be burned. But you don't need a law against arson when there are no arsonists about.

We have laws against robbery, murder, rape, and speeding. But we still have robberies, killings, rapes, and folk driving over the speed limit.

67

When I had spoken on this theme in an Ohio city the chief of detectives approached me and said, "What you said makes sense. People are always breathing down the cops' necks, but what they forget is that the law cannot operate until *after* the crime has been committed. Laws cannot deter men from doing wrong; they can only punish the wrong-doer." He paused, then added, "If we are ever to get rid of crime, we'll have to begin sometime, somewhere, before the commitment of crime."

The Apostle Paul might have agreed with the man. He said, "If there had been a law given which could have given life, verily righteousness should have been by the law."[1] And long before Paul, the Greek philosopher, Aristotle, said, "The law has no power to command obedience."

Some men will commit crime in spite of all laws — and there are over a million laws on the statute books in the United States alone! Some men would not do wrong if the million statutes were taken *off* the books.

Once I posed this question to an audience: "Suppose the law against theft was suspended tomorrow from 7.00 A.M. to 7:00 P.M., and you were free to steal all day; how many of you would go out and steal something? If you would, please lift your hands." Not a hand was raised! Granted we may have had a sprinking of liars in the crowd, still I was ready to believe that in that particular audience few of them would steal even if the law against larceny were repealed. Why? They just weren't thieves! The law against larceny was made for thieves, not for honest men. "The law," says Paul, "is not made for a righteous man, but for the lawless and disobedient."[2] You can't put it any plainer than that. The law is for outlaws. Who else? Law-abiding men don't need it. It doesn't help good men be good; it only hangs a threat over the head of the bad man.

Even the Law of God — to say nothing of the laws of men — cannot save us. It can only condemn us when we have violated it. Hence the Law can never make us righteous. It cannot make us love others.

Our need is for an inward urgency toward principles enjoined by the Law. The Law is like a mirror that a man looks into, seeing what manner of man he is; but the mirror cannot change the man one way or another. Said Paul to the Romans, "God has done what the Law, weakened here by the flesh, could not do; by sending his own Son in the guise of sinful flesh, to deal with sin . . . in order to secure the fulfilment of the Law's requirements in our lives, as we live and move, not by the flesh but by the Spirit."[3]

The way out of lawlessness is not by enacting more laws. Too few would be better than many which we don't keep! Nor will the evolving of a "new morality" help us — for such a move is aimed at helping us *by-pass* the old principles. Not even a heroic resolution, or a Herculean effort, to keep the old just laws are enough. This way lies legalism, a pretense of doing something without the heart being in it. Jesus warned us against the badness of such "goodness." He called men "actors" who were legalists. He said they were tombs, outwardly beautiful but "full of dead men's bones" within. He charged that the *act* of adultery was not needed to make a man guilty; only a look was sufficient. Killing someone wasn't necessary to make a killer; hate would do. For we are made right, not by an outward law, but by an inward spirit. A miracle must happen to a man, by God's grace. Then only could he sing — and really mean it: — "I delight in thy Law, O Lord." Then only would the law be no longer a foe, but a friend.

A well-known movie star, who had been under heavy

criticism because of her escapades, said, "In all my life, despite everything that has been said about me, I've never hurt a living soul, or broken up a home, or stolen another woman's husband."

Is it possible one can feel self-righteous because he has not stolen another's mate, or robbed a bank, or stabbed someone with a knife? It seems so. We once asked a man if he were a Christian and he informed us that he was not a thief, a drunk, or a wife-beater. He was just staying out of jail! But, somehow, for this reason he was calling himself a Christian.

Living by standards they set for themselves some folk try to be Christians rather cheaply. They ignore the fact that one's not being an outright criminal has nothing to do with being a disciple of Christ. I have known any number of unbelievers who did not drink, gamble or rob their neighbors. In fact some of the nicest people I've met knew practically nothing about the Gospel of Christ.

Evidently some folk think that attending a religious service, or performing a ritual, will make them Christians. One wonders where such ideas came from, seeing they are so foreign to New Testament teaching. In that Book we are confronted with the demand made to Nicodemus — "Ye must be born again." We are told by Paul we must be new creations, must be "crucified with Christ." We must "walk in newness of life."

We discover individuals who apparently think that because they are not associated with a non-Christian group they are Christians! I asked one fellow if he were a Christian, and he said, "I'm not a Buddhist!" I hadn't asked him if he were a Buddhist. Should I ask a man, "Are you a Frenchman?" I might be rather confused if he said, "I'm not an Irishman!"

Persons who depend on their negative goodness often over-rate their own righteousness. The movie star who boasted that she had never stolen another woman's husband says, "In all my life I've never hurt a living soul!" Now, that would be an impressive testimony — if it were true. But it isn't. Who lives who hasn't at some time hurt someone?

It's always interesting to see that those who have little real righteousness are prone to parade what they do have in such a fine manner. Witness the Pharisees in Jesus' day. Yet He found them anything but righteous in the sight of God. The truly good man is humbled by the knowledge of how terrible he would be without God's grace. One of the best men ever to live said, "Christ Jesus came into the world to save sinners, of whom I am chief."

Nothing tosses up a roadblock between a man and his Creator more than man's pride in his own worth. What is sin basically but human pride? Pride puts forth its fruit — which fruit the New Testament condemns — self-reliance, self-knowledge, self-goodness. The New Testament insists that men by their own wisdom do not know God; by their self-sufficiency they rule God out of their lives; and by their self-righteousness they reject the righteousness which is in God's Son.

It is common knowledge that the Alcoholics Anonymous will not attempt to reform a drunkard until he admits he cannot save himself. Just so long as he persists in thinking he has strength to quit the jug he cannot be helped. His only hope is to admit his hopelessness!

So it is with a man who would be saved from his sins and made acceptable to the Lord; he must surrender his own righteousness, which the Bible dubs as "filthy rags." (What a thing to say about that which a man prizes so

highly!) Paul told the Philippians that he was not count-
ing on his own righteousness, that he classed it as "garbage,"
in order that he might have the "righteousness which is of
God by faith." We cannot live unto God until we have
died unto ourselves. We are never right when we are
right in our own eyes; but only when we are right in the
eyes of God.

Self-goodness builds the highest wall between the soul
and God. Who could forget the story Jesus told of the
Pharisee and the publican who went into the Temple to
pray? One man catalogued his virtues before God! The
other pounded his breast in an agony of sorrow over his
wrongs and groaned, "God be merciful to me, a sinner!"
That man, said Jesus, was the better of the two. He had
a chance with God; the other didn't.

One man said, "I was always a nice boy, but my
brother was incorrigible. He really went bad. He drank
and stole and wound up in jail. I was troubled about him,
but I felt rather smug regarding my own fine life. Actually, I was a self-righteous snob and didn't realize it! I
was *so* ashamed of my brother, who had been in jail. He
was a rotter! And my own life was good.

"Then, once when I was reading about the prodigal
son in the Bible the truth hit me hard — the fact that the
emphasis in that story was on the self-righteousness of the
son who had never sunk into the depths from which his
brother was saved by a father's love. The smug son in the
parable stood in the dark, feeling sorry for himself because
someone had found out how wonderful love is; and he was
missing the music and the feast, while the forgiven bad boy
was having the time of his life!

"That truth put be on my face. I saw myself as bad
as my jail-bird brother. Mine was an insufferable sort of

wickedness because it was so associated with selfishness. I asked mercy from God, and found it. My filthy rags fell off and I was another man. My dab of righteousness over which I'd been so vain was like Paul's 'garbage.' The wonderful righteousness which I found in Christ left me awed and deeply humbled.

"In my new state of mind and soul I was no longer ashamed of my brother; I felt for him a deep compassion. And what is more, with my new attitude, I was able to bring him to the Lord also!"

Genuine righteousness is never reached save on the road of genuine humility. A man's first step toward being a Christian is his recognition of his own unworthiness and sinfulness — regardless of his personal virtues — in the sight of One whose holiness is beyond our comprehension. Thus cast down we may be lifted up. Hopeless, we find hope. Knowing our lostness, we may be found. Aware that we are sinners, we become aware that Christ died for sinners. Confessing our status we come to the gate of the Kingdom. For we are saved by grace.

If we seem to stress the personal life of a man, remember we are discussing the way out of our lamentable human situation. We cannot escape from it by seizing on "new" ethical codes, thinking to scrap the old one; nor by setting up "new" laws; or by assuming a respect for the old laws that we do not really possess. We are, through sin, outlaws — "All have sinned and come short of the glory of God." We must surrender to God on His own terms; we must end our rebellion utterly and completely. We must accept His government and take His ways. His reign must begin in our hearts.

11. THE KINGDOM IN THE HEART

First, then, if we would be saved in our terrifying human situation, we must break with our ancient outlawry and cast our lot forever with our Creator and Redeemer. We are wasting our time hatching up new "ethics," or planning schemes pleasing to God's old enemy, the devil. We must make a clean break with all human pride, and humble our arrogant human wills.

Freed from our mutiny against God and His Law we enter upon a new citizenship. "Now that we have been justified through faith," Paul writes to the Romans, "let us continue at peace with God."[1] Indeed, let us do so! The Enemy has become our ally. We have put down the arms of rebellion and walk, free from the dreadful battle, under banners of love. The war is over! We are "at peace" with God and with His sovereign reign.

But is this all — the end of the war? By no means. We have also the peace *of* God. "The peace of God, which passeth all understanding, shall keep your hearts and minds through Christ Jesus."[2]

Yet still there is more. We "follow peace with all men."[3] Christians are peace-lovers, not peace-breakers. They are not rioters, looters, brick-slingers, rapists. They are never part of the mindless mobs, unrestrained and mutinous, urged on by blind hate. Christians love order and decency, for theirs is a God of Order; they respect others' rights, and long to dwell in peace with their fellowmen.

Christians honor the Law. They respect the laws of man because they know the Law of God has ordained them, and they delight in the Law of God. His Law is written not only in a statute book, but is engraved on the inner soul. The Lord promised, "I will put my laws into their hearts, and in their minds will I write them."[4] He has kept that promise.

Ours might be a time, once again, with the existential trumpets ringing in our ears, to re-examine the personal and social aspects of our Gospel in the light of what Jesus taught and did — although our theme appears rather worn out from use by now!

There are not, of course, two Gospels, one personal, the other social. The Gospel is one. A person cannot have an individual experience with Christ without making some impact on the society wherein he moves.

We stray far afield from Jesus' teachings when we become so involved with saving society that we forget about saving ourselves. For us to launch any reformation of society without being ourselves regenerated is an attempt to save the world in the same manner as the world is trying to save itself! If Jesus taught anything He taught that the world, without Him, could never be saved.

"Good legislature cannot be enforced finally," said a prominent jurist, "without a good public conscience." How shall we attain to this conscience? Education? A Methodist bishop has pointed out that even *Christian* education is a failure unless the individual personally accepts God, and is *aware that he has been accepted of God.* This experience is basic to creating good conscience.

We must never shut our eyes and ears to the honest cry that the Church has often been betrayed and retarded by those who say, "Lord, Lord," and do little about God's will. Actual Christianity cannot end in an "experience" — although it begins with one. Still we are constantly confronted in the New Testament by the fact that Jesus and His followers put vast stress on a man's personal spiritual encounter with God.

Perhaps few religious institutions ever needed reformation more than did the one headed by the Pharisees. Yet when the Master met one of their chiefs by night, rather than asking for a sweeping reform in the organization, He reminded the leader that his supreme need was a personal "new birth."

Picture a world half-slave, blighted with drunkenness, torn with racial strife, immersed in political corruption, troubled with wars and rumors of wars. Imagine then a religious leader rising in the midst of that world and never delivering a single sermon against any of these things! That's how it was with Jesus. A person searches in vain for one message from Him on slavery, the liquor traffic, racial discrimination, war, or bad politics.

Certainly He stood opposed to all these things. Listening to His Word we get the feeling that He is promising that these things may be abolished — if men will take His Gospel seriously! But no human magic or panacea will work collectively on men. Jesus insisted that "out of the heart" marched the evils that corrupt the world.

Not by precept only, but by example, did Jesus lay

stress on the need for individual spiritual renewal. Take a classic New Testament picture: A wild nudist is loose in the hills. The Master meets him. What a fine chance to go clamoring for legislation to squash all nudists! But Legion needed more than a new suit — much as we think he should have been wearing some clothing! He had something fearfully wrong with him within. He had demon trouble. A change had to be made in the fellow's mysterious inner being. The devils had to go! And they went, at the Master's command. Then the man reached for a garment. He was soon "clothed, and in his right mind."[5]

Have you never asked yourself if this world is in its right mind? Were we truly sane would we carry on as we do? Sin is more dreadful than our "civilized" minds have imagined. Against the cataclysmic evil of this era we surely need a social gospel! But could such a gospel exist, with dynamic enough to level our dark tides, unless it began in that laboratory where motives are made — the human heart? And we are right back where Jesus started with Nicodemus — we must be born again. And masses are not born — save person by person.

Take another New Testament story: The treasurer of the primitive church watched a woman who, out of an agony of devotion to her Master, anointed Him with costly perfume. Judas was immediately concerned with "the poor." Marx-like, he must save the downtrodden! (How many political causes have been made, using the "poor" for pawns!) This perfume, saturating the room with its testimony of a woman's love for her Lord, could procure soup for the hungry proletariat.

Jesus not only penetrated Judas' materialistic mask; He left a message for men to remember: personal devotion to Him is important! Without it, indeed, the social gospel collapses. The love for mankind is blessed; but the Apostle Paul said it was the *love of Christ* that urged him toward trying to effect mankind's redemption.

I was in Montgomery, Alabama, when the first wave of "freedom riders" came. A frail-looking preacher of the Gospel, who ministered in the state jails and had brought many men, both Negro and white, to the Lord, faced one "rider" and asked, "Why have you come?"

"I am here in Christ's name," said the man.

"Have you come in His name only, or in His Spirit? We have too many here already who do not have His Spirit! If Christ is not Lord of your life you may as well go back. If we cannot make Christ a living reality in both the black man and the white, then their war will never end!"

We are not bound to agree with that jail-worker, of course. But will *any* of our wars ever end without the regeneration of men, and a vaster commitment to Him than we have ever yet known?

We repeat: our theme is old and time-worn. Still, the agonizing ages have seen reformation after reformation, law after law passed. We have social enterprises unnumbered. We have the United Nations. We have ecumenical councils. But the wars go on. Racial strife continues, not merely skin against skin, but the white man against the white, the black against the black. Social ills and evils are not abolished. Christ's Word is like a terrible cry in our world: *without me ye can do nothing!*

But how can we have Him socially, politically or economically if we do not have Him personally? He cannot move in our society unless He lives in our hearts. And this is no less a truth because it has been said ten thousand times!

I heard a clergyman speak disparagingly of Billy Graham's Gospel of individual redemption; but I suggested he re-check and see if *his* program was creating a greater Christian consciousness and conscience in human society than Graham's. He might well check also and see what Jesus said about a tiny seed becoming a giant tree.

Graham is at least getting men to Christ. Isn't that what Jesus asked us to do? Jesus never boasted that He would get the whole world saved, but He did promise to save all who came to Him. Only that part of society will be redeemed that desires redemption. To date the unredeemed outnumber the redeemed outrageously. What society could properly function with a minority saved and a majority lost? Again we have completed a circle. We are back to where Jesus said to a lone member of a decadent religious group: "*You* must be born again!"

12. THE LAST BEST HOPE

We have considered the law of both man and God. We know that both may be broken. Therefore the law itself cannot save us. It cannot save either our souls or our society. For lawlessness comes from lawless hearts.

We have examined man's attempt to by-pass the law by introducing a "new morality." This is, as we have said, simply the *old immorality;* just another way to violate the law and ease our conscience while we do it.

Many evil men make no bones about their lawlessness. Others salute it hypocritically while breaking it. Still others try valiantly to keep it and often fail at some point. How then shall we resolve the conflict?

The Apostle Paul has the answer. "Christ is an end to the law, so as to let every believer have righteousness."[1] Paul goes further: "If righteousness comes by law, then Christ died for nothing."[2] He goes further still: "The fruit of the Spirit is love, joy, peace, longsuffering, gentleness, goodness, faith, meekness, temperance: *against such there is no law.*"[3]

81

Paul, then, has one answer to our disorder and anarchy: *Christ!*

In fact, this is the one answer of the whole New Testament. It was the answer of the primitive Church. It should be the answer of the Church today. It is the only answer we have. All the other answers are mocking questions.

Of course, this answer will be derided by many as "oversimplification" — a rather abused and battered word in this generation. It sounds so uncomplicated, this offering Christ to a complicated human race.

One man asked: "Can Christ save the world?"

I once knew a gifted man, a clergyman who spoke to big crowds. But one day he resigned from his pulpit. He gave up his faith and said, "I have reached the conclusion that Christianity can never save this earth." A friend of mine said to him, "Electricity cannot light up a house if the tenant refuses to have it turned on!"

It is easy to point out that Christ has failed to save the world. The truth is, of course, that the world has failed Christ. A man cannot blame his physician for failing to cure him when he refuses to have the prescription filled.

The New Testament is clear on Christ's mission to the world. He came to bear witness to the truth. He came to seek and to save the lost. He came to be the light of the world. He came to give men eternal life. But that was only *His* part in God's plan for redemption. Man has a part, too.

The words of Jesus fall sadly on history — "Ye would not come to me that ye might have life."[4] He came to save His people from their sins; but that is precisely what they did not *want!* They wanted to keep their sins and hang onto their delusions. They loved darkness rather than light.

The people wanted a miracle-worker who was also a King on a lifted throne. They desired a Messiah who would crush all their enemies and make them the dominant people of the earth. They asked for trumpets, and parades, and big parties. They did not relish a Messiah with scuffed shoes and no place to put down His head!

You can't very well save people who don't wish to be saved. It's impossible to give light to the mole who burrows into the blackness at the first sign of light. What good is truth for one who loves lies and clasps evil to his breast?

"I came that they might have life," said Jesus.[5] But ask the doctor about the patient who does not want to get well. Many a person has died who might have recovered if he had had the will to live. Christ has done His part and finished His work. You can write over the cross: "Mission Accomplished." So — we are liberated, freed from the manacles of sin. I once heard of a convict who was freed from prison, but the problem of living free in the world frightened him. He went back and begged the officials to return him to his cell. No man is free who does not will his own freedom, though he be legally free.

My friend who quit the pulpit was right — Christ cannot save the world! Not unless the world will be saved. To be sure, Christ *does* save men. He has saved uncounted thousands. They will stand in an innumerable throng before His throne and praise Him as their Redeemer; so prophesy the Scriptures. But while this throng was being redeemed, a much larger throng, doubtless, was being lost. For Christ's redemption is not inescapable! Christ could have saved Herod — yet He didn't. Herod wouldn't have it that way. The Gospel failed to save Agrippa, and many others. Penicillin cannot cure pneumonia when it is barred from the patient's body. Grace can save us only when grace is accepted by us.

Men are ready to accept a Saviour who will fit into their scheme of things; who will adapt Himself to their philosophy. They will have Him as a Teacher, providing they can throw out whatever part of His teachings with which they disagree. They will accept Him as an Example, if He will not lead them in ways too rough. Numberless persons delight in Jesus' parables, thrill to His poetry, repeat His prayer, salute His greatness; but ask them to let Him save them from their sins, turn from the wrong and death, receive the Truth — and watch the congregation thin out!

Many a man, to be sure, will agree to be saved from his sins — if he can still keep them. When God asks him to confess, renounce and forsake his sins he is as cooperative as a cat being given a bath.

Others are quite willing to give up their sins, for their sins have dragged them down to a frightful state; they wish to escape the little hell they have made for themselves. But ask them to make a complete surrender to Christ, to be charged with His Spirit, to serve Him in His Kingdom — and the air is thick with excuses!

Let us face it. Christ cannot save a world that likes what it's doing without Him. He cannot save a world that prefers the wages of sin to the gift of God. He cannot redeem a world that thinks it can redeem itself. He cannot impart His righteousness to those who trust in their own righteousness. He cannot regenerate men who love a dollar-sign above the cross.

Christ cannot save the world — the world *sees* to that! But it is the world that fails, not Christ. Let no man deceive himself — Christ is still the world's Saviour. Ask the blundering fisherman from Galilee. Ask the energetic apos-

tle to the Gentiles. Ask a million men who have found
eternal life in accepting Christ's Word. Christ *could* save
the world. The world will have to answer in God's judgment if He fails to save it!

We have talked of how things are. But things are not
as they should be.

There should be peace in the world. Men should love
each other. Sin does not suit us — we were made for something better. An old question stabs at us out of the New
Testament — "What sort of people ought you to be?"[6] We
ought to be altogether different from what we are.

The Sermon on the Mount gives us an idea of what our
goal should be. For twenty centuries we have been haunted
by One whose life represents the sort of lives we should
live. Within our secret, sinful, stubborn hearts we know
He is right about things. And when we drop our gadgets
and gimmicks and noise-making and strutting long enough
to sit down and really think about things we know we'll
never be what we ought to be until we let Him move into
the living room of our lives. We knock ourselves out with
booze, we chase other men's women, we gamble, we con-
nive and conspire with evil, we parade and loot and scream
in our streets — trying to forget what Christ has called us
to be.

His cross looks down at us, and we look away. His
Word leaps at us from a thousand tongues, and we stop
our ears. He stalks our tormented earth on Love's feet
and holds out Love's hands to us, despite the fact that we
are little and cheap and selfish and stupid in our sin.

We know the truth. We run from it every day. It
troubles our dreams and nags us in our time awake. We
know the truth — that we can *never* have a right world

without letting Him be our Master! We know He is the last and best hope we have, or will ever have.

What in heaven's name are we waiting for?

Anti-Christ?

It just could be. Time is running out on us. We had better check the clock. It may not be just a gag that it's later than we think. It may *be* that late!

13. THE REAL QUESTION

Although it may be like calling down on our heads the charge of "obscurantism," we feel that the survival or death of our world shall be determined by our answer to an old question. Jesus put that question, not only to the argumentative Pharisees, but to all the ages that should come after Him.

What think ye of Christ?

One's approach to this question may be more difficult than some men imagine. To respond to it as Jesus would have us respond may mean something of a spiritual death march for us, a self-dying, a surrender of our most prized human possession: pride. To properly answer the question we would have to become, as Jesus suggested, like little children. We would have to recognize and accept the awful sovereignty of the Almighty, and His will in the matter of saving mankind "by the foolishness of preaching" the Gospel. And it would require that "leap of faith" referred to by Kierkegaard.

This would not be easy — man being what he is. For he is stubbornly wrong, not right; amazingly evil, not good. The bent away from Truth is greater than we think. We harbor more hell than we imagine. We hate God much worse than we admit. We reject Christ harder than we know. We are fearfully and wonderfully made — and dreadfully susceptible to sin. We lie to ourselves with ingenuity! We deceive ourselves so successfully!

What think ye of Christ?

To be sure, men have long thought about Him; He has thrust Himself irresistibly into the world's mind. Even in this time of dark apostasy in the church, and of the rejection of the church by the world, we must think about Him — philosopher, historian, scientist, theologian. And as in the days when He walked the earth, some, after thinking on Him, would crucify Him; others would die for Him. But far more would put Him on a cross than give Him their lives!

The New Testament reports on what men thought of Him. Some maintained He was a *bad* man. The Romans saw Him as an enemy of the state, as do the communists today. The Pharisees and Saducees saw Him as an enemy of the church. The church chieftains were especially needled by His testimony that He and His Father were one. This made Him in their eyes a renegade and blasphemer; He was an affront to the God they worshiped. This made Him not only undesirable, but dangerous. What if the crowd ever decided to go along with such nonsense? That could ruin the church, uproot institutional religion — even bring down the judgment of God upon them!

So to them Jesus was an evil man, false prophet; even worse, a false messiah. Small wonder He ate with publicans and sinners! He was of their stripe. That was where He belonged, with the riffraff and irresponsible unwashed of the world. What was frightening to them was that Jesus was *not* just another faceless fool in the mob; He was different! He was a thunderous voice. He did remarkable things. He was getting a following. He was filling the heads of the people with wild dreams. He might well bring down the anger of Caesar on them!

Others in Jesus' day saw Him as a *madman*. Only a mentally disturbed fellow could make such outlandish statements as He made! Consider the remark — "Before Abraham was, I am!" Into what delusions of grandeur could a mind reach before it could utter such a testimony? Then there was that ridiculous thing He said: "He that believeth on me, though he were dead, yet shall he live!" He had gone so far as to challenge them that if they killed Him He had power to take up His life again.

Still others saw Jesus as the *God-man*. This was what He claimed for Himself. He put His challenge squarely to them, saying that if they couldn't believe His words, then they should believe Him because of His works. Indeed, they saw astounding things. His was a power they had never witnessed in other men. He bore authority that was both comforting and frightening. How could you disregard a Man who could call back the dead, or make a hurricane lie down like a pet dog? Who could feed five thousand people with five loaves?

Other things about Him could not be brushed off: His holiness, His insight into man's nature, His knowledge of God. Small wonder one of them finally cried out, "Thou art the Christ, the Son of the living God!"

Today, in a far different world, with thunder overhead and in the earth and oceans underneath, we are still forced to think about this Man from Nazareth. To some He is still evil, to others mad. To others He is the God-man.

If He is other than what He claims to be, then His critics are right who think He is either bad or mad. But if He is all He claims to be we are still confronted with the most amazing fact in the world: God's invasion of human history as a personal Redeemer; God, becoming Justifier of the unjust, Saviour of the ungodly. The Greeks called that insanity; for how irrational it sounds before "the wisdom of this world"! It mocks our legal systems, makes havoc of our human judgments! Yet this is precisely what the Gospel teaches. "He was made sin for us, who knew no sin, that we might be made the righteousness of God in Him." If Christ is not what His critics claim, then He is what His followers claim; and if He is what they claim, then this is the doing of God, and it is marvelous in our eyes! If this be God's way, then all other ways are dead-end streets: and man's vaunted "reason" which opposes God, as well as the irrational subjectivism of existentialism which disowns God, is a disillusion and a snare. If Christ *is* the light of the world, and Christ is refused, then mankind has nothing to look forward to but Night.

What think ye of Christ?

There are many things to think about in this thunderous moment in history: the threat of a global nuclear halocaust, international revolutions, the explosive doctrines of dangerous young minds, the escalation of crime that threatens to engulf us in anarchy, apostasy from spiritual standards, declension from moral laws, the almost insufferable confusion that grips the nations of the earth. But if we will not think, and in the right way, about Christ, then soon it may not matter what any of us think about any of these things!

APPENDIX

CHAPTER 2

1. Matthew 24:9
2. II Thessalonians 2:4
3. Revelation 13:6-8
4. Colossians 2:8 (New English Bible)

CHAPTER 3

1. Hosea 4:6
2. Deuteronomy 33:2, 3
3. Isaiah 51:4
4. Habakkuk 1:3, 4 (Moffatt)
5. Daniel 2:21 (Moffatt)
6. Matthew 22:21
7. Romans 13:1-7 (Phillips)
8. I Peter 2:13-17 (Phillips)
9. Proverbs 25:5; 28:2, 3 (Moffatt)
10. Acts 5:29
11. Matthew 5:17
12. Psalm 111:7, 8

CHAPTER 4

1. Isaiah 47:3
2. Nahum 3:5
3. Revelation 3:18

CHAPTER 5

1. Romans 1:25
2. Matthew 5:43
3. John 9:31
4. Romans 1:23
5. II Thessalonians 2:10-12
6. Hebrews 6:18 (A.S.V.)

CHAPTER 6

1. Matthew 16:12
2. Matthew 7:28
3. John 7:16

4. I Timothy 4:11
5. I Timothy 4:6
6. Isaiah 32:6
7. Hebrews 13:9

CHAPTER 7

1. James 2:19
2. Matthew 8:29
3. Luke 4:41
4. Acts 19:15
5. Mark 1:25; 5:7
6. Luke 10:17-20
7. Mark 1:26
8. Matthew 12:45
9. Mark 9:18
10. I Timothy 4:1
11. Matthew 9:33
12. Acts 16:16
13. Ephesians 6:12
14. Matthew 17:18
15. Matthew 12:45; Luke 8:2

CHAPTER 8

1. Hosea 5:10
2. Lamentations 2:4
3. Deuteronomy 29:24
4. Zephaniah 3:8 (Moffatt)
5. Matthew 25:41
6. Romans 1:18
7. Romans 2:8
8. Ephesians 5:4-6
9. I Thessalonians 2:16 (Moffatt)
10. Revelation 6:17
11. Psalm 78:49, 50 (Moffatt)

CHAPTER 10

1. Galatians 3:21
2. I Timothy 1:9
3. Romans 8:3, 4 (Moffatt)

CHAPTER 11

1. Romans 5:1 (N.E.B.)
2. Philippians 4:7

3. Hebrews 12:14
4. Hebrews 10:16
5. Luke 8:26-36

CHAPTER 12

1. Romans 10:4 (Moffatt)
2. Galatians 2:21 (N.E.B.)
3. Galatians 5:22, 23
4. John 5:39
5. John 10:10
6. II Peter 3:11 (Phillips)